Pray the ROSARY

HOW TO SAY THE ROSARY

THE Apostles' Creed is said on the Crucifix; the Our Father is said on each of the Large Beads; the Hail Mary on each of the Small Beads; the Glory Be to the Father after the three Hail Marys at the beginning of the Rosary, and after each group of Small Beads.

ROSARY INDULGENCES

A plenary indulgence is granted, if the Rosary is recited in a church or public oratory or in a family group, a religious Community or pious Association; a partial indulgence is granted in other circumstances.

The gaining of the plenary indulgence is regulated by the following norms:

1) The recitation of a fourth part only of the Rosary suffices; but the five decades must be recited continuously.

2) The vocal recitation must be accompanied by pious meditation on the Mysteries.

3) In public recitation the Mysteries must be announced in the manner customary in the place; for private recitation, however, it suffices if the recitation is accompanied by meditation on the Mysteries.

. . . .
Name

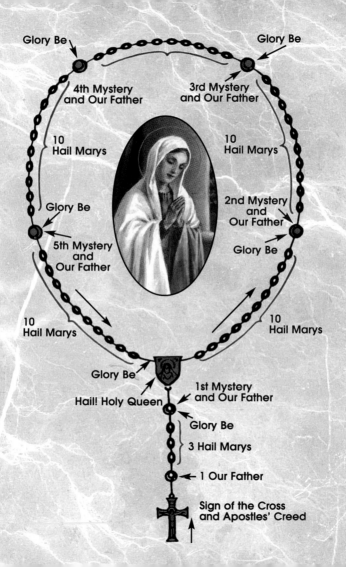

Glory Be

Glory Be

4th Mystery
and Our Father

3rd Mystery
and Our Father

10
Hail Marys

10
Hail Marys

Glory Be

2nd Mystery
and
Our Father

5th Mystery
and Our Father

Glory Be

10
Hail Marys

10
Hail Marys

Glory Be

1st Mystery
and Our Father

Hail! Holy Queen

Glory Be

3 Hail Marys

1 Our Father

Sign of the Cross
and Apostles' Creed

*Our Lady of the Rosary
of Fatima*

New Expanded Edition of

Pray the
ROSARY

for
ROSARY NOVENAS
FAMILY ROSARY
PRIVATE RECITATION
FIVE FIRST SATURDAYS

Preface by
Rev. Patrick Peyton C.S.C.

CATHOLIC BOOK PUBLISHING CORP.
NEW JERSEY

Preface

I HOPE that this beautiful little book will be your guide to a richer and more intimate understanding of the Holy Rosary.

Keep it handy in your home and in your pocket or purse, because it is an inspiration to loving meditation on the Mysteries of Our Lord Jesus as you address Our Blessed Lady in petition and thanksgiving.

May Jesus and Mary bless all who use it with tender and personal devotion.

Father Patrick Peyton, C.S.C.

NIHIL OBSTAT:
  Rev. Msgr. James M. Cafone, M.A., S.T.D.
  Censor Librorum
IMPRIMATUR:
  ✚ Most Rev. John J. Myers, J.C.D., D.D.
  Archbishop of Newark

(T-52)

ISBN 978-0-89942-052-3

RELIGIOUS devotion, public or private, for the duration of nine days to gain special graces, is called a Novena. Those who perform it with a lively hope of having their request granted, and with perfect resignation should it be refused, may be assured that Christ will grant some grace or blessing, though in His infinite wisdom and mercy He may refuse the particular favor which they implore.

Novenas originated in imitation of the Apostles who were gathered together in prayer for nine days from the time of Our Lord's Ascension to Pentecost Sunday. However, care must be taken lest the power of any Novena be limited to the number *nine* rather than perseverance in fervent prayer.

The practice of saying the Rosary nine times in the form of a Rosary Novena in *petition* or *thanksgiving* is another way of heeding Our Lady of Fatima's admonition to *Pray the Rosary*.

The 54 Day Novena Devotion, which originated in 1884 at the Sanctuary of Our Lady of the Rosary of Pompei, consists of the daily recitation of five decades of the Rosary for twenty-seven days in *petition* and five decades for twenty-seven additional days in *thanksgiving*. In reality you will be making three Novenas *in petition* for *a particular favor* and three Novenas *in thanksgiving* for a *particular favor*.

1st day say the 5 Joyful Mysteries.

2nd day say the 5 Sorrowful Mysteries.

3rd day say the 5 Glorious Mysteries.

4th day begin again the 5 Joyful Mysteries, etc.*

---

* *Note:* the new Luminous Mysteries recommended by Pope John Paul II in his pastoral letter on October 16, 2002 could be inserted in this Novena on the 2nd day, dropping the Sorrowful and the Glorious Mysteries each one day (to the 3rd and 4th days respectively). The Joyful Mysteries could begin again on the 5th day.

*The Family That Prays Together . . .
Stays Together*

THE Family Rosary is the Rosary recited *aloud together*, by as many of the family and their friends as can be present, or even by only two. Any family may say the Family Rosary in any suitable place and at any time.

A leader says aloud the first part of each prayer; a second person or group of persons answers aloud the second part of that prayer.

To begin the Family Rosary, all hold the Crucifix of their Rosary in the right hand and make the Sign of the Cross.

The leader begins the Apostles' Creed and proceeds to say the Our Father on the large beads and the Hail Mary on the small beads. The leader announces the Mystery before each decade. Five decades should be recited each day.

THE FIVE FIRST SATURDAYS

Mary's Great Promise at Fatima

THE Five First Saturdays are intended to honor and to make reparation to the Immaculate Heart of Mary for all the blasphemies and ingratitude of people.

This devotion and the wonderful promises connected with it were revealed by the Blessed Virgin at Fatima, a small village in Portugal. Our Lady appeared to three children there in 1917, and one of the little girls, Lucy, tells us that she said: *I promise to help at the hour of death, with the graces needed for salvation, whoever on the First Saturday of five consecutive months shall:*

1. *Confess and receive Communion;*

2. *Recite five decades of the Rosary;*

3. *And keep me company for fifteen minutes while meditating on the twenty Mysteries of the Rosary, with the intention of making reparation to me.*

PRAYER BEFORE
THE ROSARY

QUEEN of the Holy Rosary, you have deigned to come to Fatima to reveal to the three shepherd children the treasures of grace hidden in the Rosary. Inspire my heart with a sincere love of this devotion, in order that by meditating on the Mysteries of our Redemption which are recalled in it, I may be enriched with its fruits and obtain peace for the world, the conversion of sinners and of Russia, and the favor which I ask of you in this Rosary. (*Here mention your request.*) I ask it for the greater glory of God, for your own honor, and for the good of souls, especially for my own. Amen.

See p. 102 for Prayer after the Rosary.

THE MYSTERIES OF THE ROSARY

The Joyful Mysteries

(Said on Mondays and Saturdays, the Sundays of Advent, and Sundays from Epiphany until Lent.)

1. **The Annunciation**
   (For the love of humility)
2. **The Visitation**
   (For charity toward my neighbor)
3. **The Nativity**
   (For love of God)
4. **The Presentation**
   (For a spirit of sacrifice)
5. **Finding in the Temple**
   (For zeal for the glory of God)

The Luminous Mysteries or Mysteries of Light

(Said on Thursdays.)

1. **The Baptism of Jesus**
   (For living my Baptismal Promises)
2. **Christ's Self-Manifestation**
   (For doing whatever Jesus says)
3. **Proclamation of the Kingdom of God**
   (For seeking God's forgiveness)
4. **The Transfiguration**
   (For becoming a new person in Christ)
5. **Institution of the Eucharist**
   (For active participation at Mass)

The Sorrowful Mysteries

(Said on Tuesdays and Fridays throughout the year; and daily from Ash Wednesday until Easter Sunday.)

1. **Agony in the Garden**
   (For true repentance for my sins)
2. **Scourging at the Pillar**
   (For a spirit of mortification)
3. **Crowning with Thorns**
   (For moral courage)
4. **Carrying of the Cross**
   (For the virtue of patience)
5. **The Crucifixion**
   (For the grace of final perseverance)

The Glorious Mysteries

(Said on Wednesdays, and the Sundays from Easter until Advent.)

1. **The Resurrection**
   (For a strong faith)
2. **The Ascension**
   (For the virtue of hope)
3. **The Descent of the Holy Spirit**
   (For zeal for the glory of God)
4. **The Assumption**
   (For the grace of a happy death)
5. **The Coronation of the B.V.M.**
   (For a greater love for Mary)

1. The Annunciation

2. The Visitation

3. The Nativity

4. The Presentation

5. Finding in the Temple

The Five
Joyful Mysteries

The Joyful Mysteries direct our mind to the Son of God, Jesus Christ, our Lord and Savior, Who took human nature from a human Mother, Mary. They also bring to our attention some of the extraordinary events that preceded, accompanied, and followed Christ's Birth

The Annunciation

◖ The Annunciation ◗

I Desire the Love of Humility

Reflection

Think of the humility of the Blessed Virgin when the Angel Gabriel greeted her with these words: "Hail, full of grace."

Participation

1 Our Father.   10 Hail Marys.
1 Glory Be to the Father.

Prayer

Mary, you received with deep humility the news of the Angel Gabriel that you were the Mother of God's Son. Obtain for me a similar *humility*.

*"O my Jesus, forgive us our sins, save us from the fire of hell, take all souls to heaven, and help especially those most in need of Your mercy."

*In her second apparition at Fatima, June 13, 1917, our Lady taught three shepherd children to add this invocation after each decade of the Rosary.

Prayer

Lord Jesus, we offer You this first decade to honor Your Incarnation, and we ask of You, through this Mystery and through the intercession of Your Holy Mother, *a deep humility of heart.*

Say 1 Our Father.

Scripture Text

Say 10 Hail Marys, each preceded by a text given below.

1. The Angel Gabriel was sent by God to a town in Galilee called Nazareth, to a virgin betrothed to a man named Joseph, of the house of David. The virgin's name was Mary.

2. The Angel came to her and said, "Hail, full of grace! The Lord is with you."

3. But she was greatly troubled by his words and wondered in her heart what this salutation could mean.

4. Then the Angel said to her, "Do not be afraid, Mary, for you have found favor with God.

5. "Behold, you will conceive in your womb and bear a Son, and you will name Him Jesus.

6. "He will be great and will be called Son of the Most High. The Lord God will give Him the throne of His ancestor David. He will rule over the house of Jacob forever, and of His Kingdom there will be no end."

7. Mary said to the Angel, "How will this be, since I am a virgin?"

8. The Angel answered, "The Holy Spirit will come upon you, and the power of the Most High will overshadow you. Therefore, the Child to be born will be holy, and He will be called the Son of God.

9. "And behold, your cousin Elizabeth in her old age has also conceived a son, and she who was called barren is now in her sixth month, for nothing will be impossible for God."

10. Then Mary said, "Behold, I am the handmaid of the Lord. Let it be done to me according to your word." After this, the Angel departed from her (Lk 1:26-38).

Additional or Alternative Text

At the end of the first part of each Hail Mary after the Name *"Jesus,"* add a few words that remind us of the Mystery being celebrated, as below. (The second part, "Holy Mary . . . ," is only recited once—at the end of the ten Hail Marys.)

(1) Who chose you as His Immaculate Mother from all eternity. **(2)** Whom the Angel Gabriel announced was to be born of you. **(3)** Whom you welcomed into your womb. **(4)** Who said "Yes" to the Father's plan to save the whole world. **(5)** Who in you accepted our poor humanity. **(6)** Who filled you with the Holy Spirit. **(7)** Who gave us a glimpse of the humility of God. **(8)** Who in you initiated the redemption. **(9)** Who made you attentive to His Word. **(10)** Who allowed you to share in His work.

Say 1 Glory Be to the Father.

May the grace of the Mystery of the Incarnation come down into my soul and make it truly humble.

"O my Jesus," etc., p. 17.

The Visitation

✆ The Visitation ✆

I Desire Charity toward My Neighbor

Reflection

Think of Mary's charity in visiting her cousin Elizabeth and remaining with her for three months before the birth of John the Baptist.

Participation

1 Our Father.   10 Hail Marys.
1 Glory Be to the Father.

Prayer

Mary, you showed true charity in visiting Elizabeth and remaining with her for three months before the birth of John the Baptist. Obtain for me the grace to *love my neighbor.*

"O my Jesus, forgive us our sins, save us from the fire of hell, take all souls to heaven, and help especially those most in need of Your mercy."

Prayer

Lord Jesus, we offer You this second decade to honor the Visitation of Your Holy Mother to her cousin St. Elizabeth, and we ask of You, through this Mystery and through Mary's intercession, *a perfect charity toward others.*

Say 1 Our Father.

Scripture Text

Say 10 Hail Marys, each preceded by a text given below.

1. Mary set out and journeyed in haste into the hill country to a town of Judah where she entered the house of Zechariah and greeted Elizabeth.

2. When Elizabeth heard Mary's greeting, the baby leaped in her womb.

3. Then Elizabeth was filled with the Holy Spirit, and she exclaimed with a loud cry, "Blessed are you among women, and blessed is the fruit of your womb.

4. "And why am I so greatly favored that the Mother of my Lord should visit me? For behold, the moment that the sound of your greeting reached my ears, the child in my womb leaped for joy.

5. "And blessed is she who believed that what the Lord has said to her will be fulfilled."

6. And Mary said, "My soul proclaims the greatness of the Lord and my spirit rejoices in God my Savior.

7. "For He has looked with favor on the lowliness of His servant; henceforth all generations will call me blessed.

8. "The Mighty one has done great things for me, and holy is His Name. His mercy is from age to age on those who fear Him. . . .

9. "He has come to the aid of Israel His servant, ever mindful of His merciful love, according to the promises He made to our ancestors, to Abraham and to his descendants forever."

10. Mary remained with Elizabeth for about three months and then returned to her home (Lk 1:39-56).

Additional or Alternative Text

At the end of the first part of each Hail Mary after the Name "*Jesus,*" add a few words that remind us of the Mystery being celebrated, as below. (The second part, "Holy Mary . . . ," is only recited once—at the end of the ten Hail Marys.)

(1) Who made you the first among believers. (2) Who in you came to visit His people. (3) Who at your greeting to Elizabeth sanctified John the Baptist in her womb. (4) Who through you blesses all expectant mothers. (5) Who visits us with His Word. (6) Who with His Body and Blood, Soul and Divinity, comes to visit us in Holy Communion. (7) Who remains silently in the Tabernacle, waiting for us to visit Him. (8) Who calls us to visit the sick. (9) Who is compassionate and all-forgiving. (10) Who with His Church sings your Gospel canticle known as the *Magnificat*.

Say 1 Glory Be to the Father.

May the grace of the Mystery of the Visitation come down into my soul and make it truly charitable.

"O my Jesus," etc., p. 17.

The Nativity

❧ The Nativity ☙

I Desire the Love of God

Reflection

Think of poverty, so lovingly accepted by Mary when she placed the Infant Jesus, our God and Redeemer, in the stable of Bethlehem.

Participation

1 Our Father.   10 Hail Marys.
1 Glory Be to the Father.

Prayer

Jesus, You lovingly accepted poverty when You were placed in a manger in the stable although You were our God and Redeemer. Grant that I may have the *love of God*.

"O my Jesus, forgive us our sins, save us from the fire of hell, take all souls to heaven, and help especially those most in need of Your mercy."

Prayer

Lord Jesus, we offer You this third decade to honor Your Birth in the stable at Bethlehem, and we ask of You, through this Mystery and through the intercession of Your Holy Mother, *sincere love of God.*

Say 1 Our Father.

Scripture Text

Say 10 Hail Marys, each preceded by a text given below.

1. When Jesus' Mother Mary was engaged to Joseph, but before they came to live together, she was found to be with child through the Holy Spirit.

2. An Angel of God appeared to Joseph in a dream and said, "Joseph, son of David, do not be afraid to receive Mary into your home as your wife. For this Child has been conceived in her womb through the Holy Spirit. She will give birth to a Son, and you shall name Him Jesus, for He will save His people from their sins." . . .

3. Joseph went from the town of Nazareth in Galilee to Judea, to the city of David called Bethlehem.

4. Because he was of the house and family of David, he went to be registered together with Mary, his betrothed, who was expecting a child.

5. While they were there, the time came for her to have a child, and she gave birth to her firstborn Son. She wrapped Him in swaddling clothes and laid Him in a manger, because there was no room for them in the inn (Lk 2:4-7).

6. In the nearby countryside there were shepherds living in the fields and keeping watch over their flock. . . .

7. Suddenly, an Angel of the Lord appeared to them, and the glory of the Lord shone around them. They were terror-stricken, but the Angel said to them, "Do not be afraid, for I bring you good news of great joy for all the people.

8. "For this day in the city of David there has been born to you a Savior Who is Christ, the Lord.

9. "This will be a sign for you: You will find an infant wrapped in swaddling clothes and lying in a manger."

10. And suddenly there was with the Angel a multitude of the heavenly host, praising God and saying, "Glory to God in the highest heaven, and on earth peace to all those on whom His favor rests" (Lk 2:8-14).

Additional or Alternative Text

At the end of the first part of each Hail Mary after the Name *"Jesus,"* add a few words that remind us of the Mystery being celebrated, as below. (The second part, "Holy Mary . . . ," is only recited once—at the end of the ten Hail Marys.)

(1) Who was the Eternal Word of God made man in a virginal birth. (2) Who was born in a lowly stable. (3) Whom you brought forth in poverty and purity. (4) Whom you nurtured and cared for with untold love. (5) Who in you redeemed all motherhood. (6) Who through you blesses the joys and pains of childbirth. (7) Whom shepherds came to adore by night. (8) Who received gifts from the Wise Men. (9) Who was persecuted by Herod. (10) Who was obliged to flee into exile.

Say 1 Glory Be to the Father.

May the grace of the Mystery of the Nativity come down into my soul and teach me to truly love God.

"O my Jesus," etc., p. 17.

The Presentation

᥈ The Presentation ᥈

I Desire a Spirit of Sacrifice

Reflection

Think of Mary's obedience to the Law of God in presenting the Child Jesus in the Temple.

Participation

1 Our Father.   10 Hail Marys.
1 Glory Be to the Father.

Prayer

Mary, you obeyed the Law of God in presenting the Child Jesus in the Temple. Obtain for me *a spirit of sacrifice*.

"O my Jesus, forgive us our sins, save us from the fire of hell, take all souls to heaven, and help especially those most in need of Your mercy."

Prayer

Lord Jesus, we offer You this fourth decade to honor Your Presentation in the Temple and the Purification of Mary, and we ask of You, through this Mystery and through her intercession, a *great spirit of sacrifice.*

Say 1 Our Father.

Scripture Text

Say 10 Hail Marys, each preceded by a text given below.

1. When the days for the purification were completed according to the Law of Moses, they brought the Child up to Jerusalem to present Him to the Lord.

2. At that time there was a man in Jerusalem whose name was Simeon. This upright and devout man was awaiting the consolation of Israel, and the Holy Spirit rested on him.

3. It had been revealed to him by the Holy Spirit that he would not experience death before he had seen the Christ of the Lord.

4. Prompted by the Spirit, Simeon came into the Temple. When the parents brought in the Child Jesus to do for Him what was required by the Law, he took Him in his arms and praised God, saying:

5. "Now, Lord, You may dismiss Your servant in peace, according to Your word.

6. "For my eyes have seen Your salvation, which You have prepared in the sight of all the peoples, a light of revelation to the Gentiles and glory for Your people Israel."

7. The Child's father and mother marveled at what was being said about Him.

8. Then Simeon blessed them and said to Mary His Mother: "This Child is destined for the fall and rise of many in Israel, and to be a sign that will be opposed, so that the secret thoughts of many will be revealed, and you yourself a sword will pierce" (Lk 2:22-35).

9. When they had fulfilled everything required by the Law of the Lord, they returned to Galilee, to their own town of Nazareth.

10. The Child grew and became strong, filled with wisdom, and God's favor was upon Him (Lk 2:39-40).

Additional or Alternative Text

At the end of the first part of each Hail Mary after the Name "*Jesus*," add a few words that remind us of the Mystery being celebrated, as below. (The second part, "Holy Mary . . . ," is only recited once—at the end of the ten Hail Marys.)

(1) Who was presented in the Temple in accord with the Law of the Lord. **(2)** Who offered a sacrifice of His humanity in this Mystery. **(3)** Who was ransomed with the offering of two turtledoves. **(4)** Who did not hide the sword of sorrows that would pierce your heart. **(5)** Who rewarded the expectation of two elderly believers, Simeon and Anna. **(6)** Who was foretold as the "Light of the Nations." **(7)** Who was proclaimed as the "Joy of His People." **(8)** Who was taken into Egypt by you and escaped Herod's plan to kill Him. **(9)** Who returned to Nazareth with you after Herod's death. **(10)** Who grew in age and wisdom.

Say 1 Glory Be to the Father.

May the grace of the Mystery of the Presentation come down into my soul and give me a spirit of sacrifice.

"O my Jesus," etc., p. 17.

Finding in the Temple

✺ Finding in the Temple ✺

I Desire Zeal for the Glory of God

Reflection

Think of the deep sorrow with which Mary sought the Child Jesus for three days, and the joy with which she found Him in the midst of the Teachers in the Temple.

Participation

1 Our Father.   10 Hail Marys.
1 Glory Be to the Father.

Prayer

Mary, you were filled with sorrow at the loss of Jesus and overwhelmed with joy on finding Him surrounded by the Teachers in the Temple. Obtain for me the *zeal for God's glory*.

"O my Jesus, forgive us our sins, save us from the fire of hell, take all souls to heaven, and help especially those most in need of Your mercy."

Prayer

Lord Jesus, we offer You this fifth decade to honor Your Finding in the Temple, and we ask of You, through this Mystery and through the intercession of Your Holy Mother, *zeal for God's glory*.

Say 1 Our Father.

Scripture Text

Say 10 Hail Marys, each preceded by a text given below.

1. Every year His parents used to go to Jerusalem for the Feast of Passover. And when Jesus was twelve years old, they made the journey as usual for the feast.

2. When the days of the feast were over and they set off for home, the Boy Jesus stayed behind in Jerusalem. His parents were not aware of this.

3. Assuming that He was somewhere in the group of travelers, they journeyed for a day. Then they started to look for Him among their relatives and friends.

4. When they failed to find Him, they returned to Jerusalem to search for Him.

5. After three days, they found Him in the Temple, where He was sitting among the Teachers, listening to them and asking them questions. And all who heard Him were amazed at His intelligence and His answers.

6. When they saw Him, they were astonished, and His Mother said to Him: "Son, why have You done this to us? Your father and I have been searching for You with great anxiety."

7. Jesus said to them, "Why were you searching for Me? Did you not know that I must be in My Father's house?"

8. But they did not comprehend what He had said to them.

9. Then He went down with them and came to Nazareth, and He was obedient to them.

10. His Mother pondered all these things in her heart. And Jesus increased in wisdom and in age and in grace with God and men (Lk 2:41-52).

Additional or Alternative Text

At the end of the first part of each Hail Mary after the Name *"Jesus,"* add a few words that remind us of the Mystery being celebrated, as below. (The second part, "Holy Mary . . . ," is only recited once—at the end of the ten Hail Marys.)

(1) Who went on pilgrimage with you and St. Joseph to the Holy City. (2) Who stayed behind in Jerusalem when you started for home. (3) Whom you sought in tears for three days. (4) Whom you and Joseph joyously found in the Temple. (5) Who was among the Teachers as their Disciple and Master. (6) Who declared Himself consecrated to the Father. (7) Who returned humbly with you to your home. (8) Who caused you to reflect upon this Mystery. (9) Whom you sought to understand. (10) Who increased in wisdom and in age and in grace with God and men.

Say 1 Glory Be to the Father.

May the grace of the Mystery of the Finding of the Child Jesus in the Temple come down into my soul and obtain for me the zeal for God's glory.

"O my Jesus," etc., p. 17.

1. The Baptism of Jesus

2. Christ's Self-Manifestation at Cana

3. Christ's Proclamation of the Kingdom

4. The Transfiguration

5. Institution of the Eucharist

The Five Luminous Mysteries

The Luminous Mysteries recall to our mind important events of the Public Ministry of Christ through which He announces the coming of the Kingdom of God, bears witness to it in His works, and proclaims its demands—showing that a Mystery of Christ is most evidently a Mystery of Light

The Baptism of Jesus

ꙮ The Baptism of Jesus ꙮ
I Desire to Live My Baptismal Promises

Reflection
Think of Christ's Baptism at the hands of John the Baptist when the Father called Him His beloved Son and the Holy Spirit descended on Him to invest Him with the mission He was to carry out.

Participation
1 Our Father.   10 Hail Marys.
1 Glory Be to the Father.

Prayer
Jesus, at Your Baptism in the Jordan, the Father called You His beloved Son and the Holy Spirit descended upon You to invest You with your mission. Help me to *keep my Baptismal Promises*.

*"O my Jesus, forgive us our sins, save us from the fire of hell, take all souls to heaven, and help especially those most in need of Your mercy."

*In her second apparition at Fatima, June 13, 1917, our Lady taught three shepherd children to add this invocation after each decade of the Rosary.

Prayer

Lord Jesus, we offer You this first decade to honor Your Baptism, and we ask of You, through this Mystery and through the intercession of Your Holy Mother, *the grace to fulfill our Baptismal Promises.*

Say 1 Our Father.

Scripture Text

Say 10 Hail Marys, each preceded by a text given below.

1. Jesus arrived from Galilee and came to John at the Jordan to be baptized by him.

2. John tried to dissuade Him, saying, "Why do You come to me? I am the one who needs to be baptized by You."

3. But Jesus said to him in reply, "For the present, let it be thus. It is proper for us to do this to fulfill all that righteousness demands."

4. Then John acquiesced.

5. After Jesus had been baptized, as He came up from the water, the heavens were opened.

6. And He beheld the Spirit of God descending like a dove and alighting on Him.

7. And a voice came from heaven, saying, "This is My beloved Son, in Whom I am well pleased."

8. [These words recall the words of the Lord spoken by the Prophet Isaiah about the Suffering Servant:]

1. The Baptism of Jesus—Long Version

"This is My Servant Whom I uphold, My chosen one in Whom I delight" (Mt 3:13-17).

9. "I will put My Spirit in Him, and He will bring justice to the nations.

10. "In His law the coastlands will place their hope. This is what the Lord says" (Isa 42:1-2, 4-5).

Additional or Alternative Text

At the end of the first part of each Hail Mary after the Name "*Jesus,*" add a few words that remind us of the Mystery being celebrated, as below. (The second part, "Holy Mary . . . ," is only recited once—at the end of the ten Hail Marys.)

(1) Who at the beginning of His Public Ministry spent forty days of fasting and prayer in the desert. (2) Who conquered the temptations put to Him by Satan. (3) Who associated Himself with those who do penance. (4) Who was baptized by John the Baptist. (5) Upon Whom the Holy Spirit descended. (6) Whom the Father identified as His beloved Son. (7) Who enables us to be born again as children of God. (8) Whom the Father revealed as the Servant of the Lord. (9) Who spoke wondrous words of wisdom when preaching. (10) Who performed stupendous miracles.

Say 1 Glory Be to the Father.

May the grace of the Mystery of Christ's Baptism come down into my soul and help me to keep my Baptismal Promises.

"O my Jesus," etc., p. 39.

Christ's Self-Manifestation at Cana

◖Christ's Self-◗ Manifestation at Cana

I Desire to Do Whatever Jesus Says

Reflection

Think of Christ's self-manifestation at the wedding of Cana when He changed water into wine and opened the hearts of the disciples to faith, thanks to the intervention of Mary, the first among believers.

Participation

1 Our Father.   10 Hail Marys.
1 Glory Be to the Father.

Prayer

Mary, the first among believers in Christ, as a result of your intercession at Cana, your Son changed water into wine and opened the hearts of the disciples to faith. Obtain for me the grace to *do whatever Jesus says.*

"O my Jesus, forgive us our sins, save us from the fire of hell, take all souls to heaven, and help especially those most in need of Your mercy."

Prayer

Lord Jesus, we offer You this second decade to honor Your Self-Manifestation at the Wedding Feast of Cana, and we ask of You, through this Mystery and through Mary's intercession, *the willingness to do whatever You say.*

Say 1 Our Father.

Scripture Text

Say 10 Hail Marys, each preceded by a text given below.

1. On the third day, there was a wedding feast at Cana in Galilee. The Mother of Jesus was there, and Jesus and His disciples had also been invited.

2. When the wine was exhausted, the Mother of Jesus said to Him, "They have no wine."

3. Jesus responded, "Woman, what concern is this to us? My hour has not yet come."

4. His Mother said to the servants, "Do whatever He tells you."

5. Standing nearby there were six stone water jugs of the type used for Jewish rites of purification, each holding twenty to thirty gallons.

6. Jesus instructed the servants, "Fill the jars with water."

7. When they had filled them to the brim, He ordered them, "Now draw some out and take it to the chief steward," and they did so.

8. When the chief steward had tasted the water that had become wine, he did not know where it came from, although the servants who had drawn the water knew.

9. The chief steward called over the bridegroom and said, "Everyone serves the choice wine first, and then an inferior vintage when the guests have had too much to drink. However, you have saved the best wine until now."

10. Jesus performed this, the first of His signs, at Cana in Galilee, thereby revealing His glory, and His disciples believed in Him (Jn 2:1-11).

Additional or Alternative Text

At the end of the first part of each Hail Mary after the Name "Jesus," add a few words that remind us of the Mystery being celebrated, as below. (The second part, "Holy Mary . . . ," is only recited once—at the end of the ten Hail Marys.)

(1) Who manifested Himself and had His mission confirmed at Cana. (2) Who listened to your request to aid the marriage couple. (3) Who, even though His hour had not yet come, changed water into the best of wines. (4) Who, by the first of His signs, revealed His glory. (5) Who thus foretold the Eucharist. (6) Who confirmed the faith of His disciples. (7) Who foretold the abundance of His Kingdom. (8) Who blesses all who come together in His Name. (9) Who intervenes in our necessities. (10) Who gave us the Sacrament of Marriage.

Say 1 Glory Be to the Father.

May the grace of the Mystery of Christ's Self-Manifestation at Cana come down into my soul and help me do whatever He tells me.

"O my Jesus," etc., p. 39.

Christ's Proclamation of the Kingdom of God

❧ Christ's Proclamation ❧ of the Kingdom of God

I Desire God's Forgiveness

Reflection

Think of Christ's preaching of the Kingdom of God with its call to forgiveness, as He inaugurated the ministry of mercy, which He continues to exercise until the end of the world, particularly through Reconciliation.

Participation

1 Our Father.   10 Hail Marys.
1 Glory Be to the Father.

Prayer

Jesus, You preached the Kingdom of God with its call to forgiveness, inaugurating the ministry of mercy, which You continue to exercise especially through the Sacrament of Reconciliation. Help me to *seek forgiveness for my sins*.

"O my Jesus, forgive us our sins, save us from the fire of hell, take all souls to heaven, and help especially those most in need of Your mercy."

Prayer

Lord Jesus, we offer You this third decade to honor Your Proclamation of the Kingdom of God, and we ask of You, through this Mystery and through the intercession of Your Holy Mother, *the pardon of all our sins*.

Say 1 Our Father.

Scripture Text

Say 10 Hail Marys, each preceded by a text given below.

1. Jesus said, "The time of fulfillment has arrived, and the Kingdom of God is close at hand. Repent, and believe in the Gospel."

2. Later, He gave them the eight Beatitudes: "Blessed are the poor in spirit, for theirs is the Kingdom of heaven.

3. "Blessed are those who mourn, for they will be comforted.

4. "Blessed are the meek, for they will inherit the earth.

5. "Blessed are those who hunger and thirst for justice, for they will have their fill.

6. "Blessed are the merciful, for they will obtain mercy.

7. "Blessed are the pure of heart, for they will see God.

8. "Blessed are the peacemakers, for they will be called children of God.

9. "Blessed are those who are persecuted in the cause of justice, for theirs is the Kingdom of heaven.

10. "Blessed are you when people insult you and persecute you and utter all kinds of calumnies against you for My sake. Rejoice and be glad, for your reward will be great in heaven" (Mk 1:14-15; Mt 5:3-12).

Additional or Alternative Text

At the end of the first part of each Hail Mary after the Name "*Jesus*," add a few words that remind us of the Mystery being celebrated, as below. (The second part, "Holy Mary . . . ," is only recited once—at the end of the ten Hail Marys.)

(1) Who was the Herald of God's Kingdom, inviting all to be converted. (2) Who gave us the Beatitudes, which have rightly been called "Eight Words for Eternity." (3) Who said the poor in spirit will attain the Kingdom. (4) Who said those who mourn will be comforted. (5) Who said the meek will inherit the earth. (6) Who said those who hunger and thirst for justice will have their fill. (7) Who said the merciful will obtain mercy. (8) Who said the pure of heart will see God. (9) Who said the peacemakers will be called children of God. (10) Who said those who are persecuted in the cause of justice will inherit the Kingdom.

Say 1 Glory Be to the Father.

May the grace of the Mystery of Christ's Proclamation of the Kingdom of God come down into my soul and take all my sins away.

"O my Jesus," etc., p. 39.

The Transfiguration

❧ The Transfiguration ❧

I Desire to Be a New Person in Christ

Reflection

Think of Christ's Transfiguration when the Glory of the Godhead shone forth from His face as the Father commanded the Apostles to listen to Him and experience His Passion and Resurrection and be transfigured by the Holy Spirit.

Participation

1 Our Father.   10 Hail Marys.
1 Glory Be to the Father.

Prayer

Jesus, at Your Transfiguration, the glory of the Godhead shone forth from Your face as the Father commanded the Apostles to hear You and be transfigured by the Holy Spirit. Help me to *be a new person in You.*

"O my Jesus, forgive us our sins, save us from the fire of hell, take all souls to heaven, and help especially those most in need of Your mercy."

Prayer

Lord Jesus, we offer You this fourth decade to honor Your Transfiguration, and we ask of You, through this Mystery and through the intercession of Your Holy Mother, *the firm desire to become new persons.*

Say 1 Our Father.

Scripture Text

Say 10 Hail Marys, each preceded by a text given below.

1. Six days later, Jesus took Peter and James and his brother John . . . with Him and led them up a high mountain by themselves.

2. And in their presence He was transfigured; His face shone like the sun, and His clothes became dazzling white.

3. Suddenly, there appeared to them Moses and Elijah, conversing with Him.

4. Then Peter said to Jesus, "Lord, it is good for us to be here.

5. "If You wish, I will make three tents here—one for You, one for Moses, and one for Elijah."

6. While he was speaking, suddenly a bright cloud cast a shadow over them.

7. Then a voice from the cloud said, "This is My Beloved Son, with Whom I am well pleased. Listen to Him."

8. When the disciples heard this, they fell on their faces and were greatly frightened.

9. But Jesus came and touched them, saying, "Stand up, and do not be frightened."

10. And when they raised their eyes, they saw no one, but only Jesus (Mt 17:1-8).

Additional or Alternative Text

At the end of the first part of each Hail Mary after the Name "*Jesus*," add a few words that remind us of the Mystery being celebrated, as below. (The second part, "Holy Mary . . . ," is only recited once—at the end of the ten Hail Marys.)

(1) Who is the Teacher of the Law and the Prophets. (2) Who journeyed with Sts. Peter, James, and John to a high mountain. (3) Who was transfigured before them—with His face shining like the sun and His clothes becoming dazzling white. (4) Who spoke with Moses (symbolizing the Law) and Elijah (symbolizing the Prophets). (5) Whom the Father called His Beloved Son and told the Apostles to listen to. (6) Who told His Apostles to stand up and not be afraid. (7) Who foretold His Resurrection. (8) Who invites us to live in a transfigured manner. (9) Who reveals in every person the image of God. (10) Who invites us to participate in the Mystery of Glory.

Say 1 Glory Be to the Father.

May the grace of the Mystery of the Transfiguration come down into my soul and make me a new person in Christ.

"O my Jesus," etc., p. 51.

Institution of the Eucharist

❧ Institution of ☙ the Eucharist

I Desire Active Participation at Mass

Reflection

Think of Christ's institution of the Eucharist, in which He offered His Body and Blood as food and drink under the signs of bread and wine and testified to His love for humanity, for whose sake He would offer Himself in sacrifice.

Participation

1 Our Father.   10 Hail Marys.
1 Glory Be to the Father.

Prayer

Jesus, at the Last Supper, You instituted the Eucharist, offering the signs of bread and wine and testifying to Your love for humanity. Help me to attain *active participation at Mass.*

"O my Jesus, forgive us our sins, save us from the fire of hell, take all souls to heaven, and help especially those most in need of Your mercy."

Prayer

Lord Jesus, we offer You this fifth decade to honor the Mystery of the Institution of the Eucharist, and we ask of You, through this Mystery and through the intercession of Your Holy Mother, *the desire to achieve active participation at every Mass.*

Say 1 Our Father.

Scripture Text

Say 10 Hail Marys, each preceded by a text given below.

1. The day of the Feast of Unleavened Bread arrived, on which the Passover lamb had to be sacrificed.

2. Jesus sent Peter and John, saying, "Go and make preparations for us to eat the Passover."

3. When the hour came, Jesus took His place at table along with the Apostles.

4. He said to them, "I have eagerly desired to eat this Passover with you before I suffer.

5. "For I tell you, that from this moment on, I shall never eat it again, until it is fulfilled in the Kingdom of God."

6. Then He took the cup, and after giving thanks, He said, "Take this and divide it among yourselves.

7. "For I tell you, that from this moment, I will not drink of the fruit of the vine until the Kingdom of God comes."

8. Then He took bread, and after giving thanks He broke it and gave it to them, saying, "This is My Body, which will be given for you.

9. "Do this in memory of Me."

10. And He did the same with the cup after supper, saying, "This cup is the new covenant in My Blood, which will be poured out for you" (Lk 22:7-8, 14-20).

Additional or Alternative Text

At the end of the first part of each Hail Mary after the Name "Jesus," add a few words that remind us of the Mystery being celebrated, as below. (The second part, "Holy Mary . . . ," is only recited once—at the end of the ten Hail Marys.)

(1) Who washed the feet of His Apostles at the Last Supper. (2) Who, as the Lord and Master of His Apostles, taught them the service of others. (3) Who sat at table with His Apostles. (4) Who gave us the greatest prayer, the Mass. (5) Who gives Himself to us under the form of food and drink. (6) Who is always with us in Tabernacles around the world. (7) Whom we come to visit and adore. (8) Who calls us to His Table. (9) Who asks us for the love of unity. (10) Whom we praise while awaiting His Second Coming.

Say 1 Glory Be to the Father.

May the grace of the Mystery of Christ's Institution of the Eucharist come down into my soul and inspire me to strive for active participation at every Mass.

"O my Jesus," etc., p. 39.

1. Agony in the Garden

2. Scourging at the Pillar

3. Crowning with Thorns

4. Carrying of the Cross

5. The Crucifixion

The Five
Sorrowful Mysteries

The Sorrowful Mysteries recall to our mind the mysterious events surrounding Christ's sacrifice of His life in order that sinful humanity might be reconciled with God

Agony in the Garden

ꙮ Agony in the Garden ꙮ

I Desire True Repentance for My Sins

Reflection

Think of our Lord Jesus in the Garden of Gethsemane, suffering a bitter agony for our sins.

Participation

1 Our Father.   10 Hail Marys.
1 Glory Be to the Father.

Prayer

Jesus, in the Garden of Gethsemane, You suffered a bitter agony because of our sins. Grant me *true contrition*.

★"O my Jesus, forgive us our sins, save us from the fire of hell, take all souls to heaven, and help especially those most in need of Your mercy."

★In her second apparition at Fatima, June 13, 1917, our Lady taught three shepherd children to add this invocation after each decade of the Rosary.

Prayer

Lord Jesus, we offer You this first decade to honor Your Mortal Agony in the Garden of Gethsemane, and we ask of You, through this Mystery and through the intercession of Your Holy Mother, *a perfect contrition for our sins*.

Say 1 Our Father.

Scripture Text

Say 10 Hail Marys, each preceded by a text given below.

1. Then they went to a place that was called Gethsemane, and Jesus said to His disciples, "Sit here while I pray."

2. He took with Him Peter and James and John, and He began to suffer distress and anguish. And He said to them, "My soul is sorrowful even to the point of death. Remain here and keep watch" (Mk 14:32-34).

3. Withdrawing from them about a stone's throw, He knelt down and prayed, "Father, if You are willing, take this cup from Me. Yet not My Will but Yours be done."

4. Then an Angel from heaven appeared to Him and gave Him strength. In His anguish, He prayed so fervently that His sweat became like great drops of blood falling on the ground (Lk 22:41-44).

5. Returning to the disciples, He found them sleeping. He said, "Simon . . . could you not keep watch for one hour? Stay awake and pray that you may not enter into temptation. The spirit is willing, but the flesh is weak."

6. Again, He went apart and prayed, saying the same words. Then He came again and found them sleeping . . . and they did not know what to say to Him.

7. When He returned a third time, He said to them, "Are you still sleeping . . . ? Enough! The hour has come when the Son of Man is to be betrayed into the hands of sinners. Get up! Let us go! Look, My betrayer is approaching. . . ."

8. At once, while Jesus was still speaking, Judas, one of the Twelve, arrived. With him there was a crowd of men armed with swords and clubs.

9. Judas proceeded directly to Jesus and said, "Rabbi!" and kissed Him.

10. Then they seized Jesus and placed Him under arrest . . . and everyone deserted Him and fled (Mk 14:37-46).

Additional or Alternative Text

At the end of the first part of each Hail Mary after the Name "*Jesus*," add a few words that remind us of the Mystery being celebrated, as below. (The second part, "Holy Mary . . . ," is only recited once—at the end of the ten Hail Marys.)

(1) Who experienced anguish in the Garden. (2) Who prayed to be free of the cup yet accepted His Father's Will. (3) Who deigned to accept consolation from an Angel. (4) Who endured a bloody sweat flowing from His sorrows. (5) Who was betrayed by a friend. (6) Who spoke to those who saw Him with the power of His Word, rendering them prostrate on the ground and then uplifted them. (7) Who told those trying to defend Him to put away the sword. (8) Who handed Himself into the hands of His enemies. (9) Who was abandoned by His Apostles. (10) Who suffered for the sins of all of us.

Say 1 Glory Be to the Father.

May the grace of our Lord's Agony come down into my soul and make me truly contrite for my sins.

"O my Jesus," etc., p. 61.

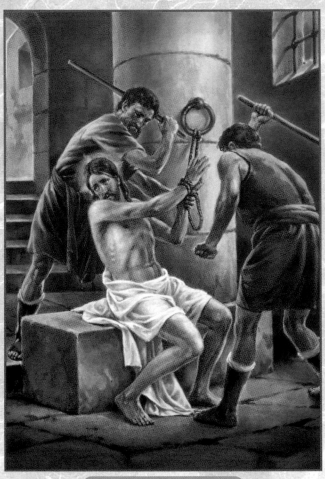

Scourging at the Pillar

❧ Scourging at the Pillar ❧

I Desire a Spirit of Mortification

Reflection

Think of the cruel scourging at the pillar that our Lord suffered and the heavy blows that tore His flesh.

Participation

1 Our Father.   10 Hail Marys.
1 Glory Be to the Father.

Prayer

Jesus, You endured a cruel scourging and Your flesh was torn by heavy blows. Help me to have *a spirit of mortification.*

"O my Jesus, forgive us our sins, save us from the fire of hell, take all souls to heaven, and help especially those most in need of Your mercy."

Prayer

Lord Jesus, we offer You this second decade to honor Your Bloody Scourging, and we ask of You, through this Mystery and through the intercession of Your Holy Mother, *the grace to mortify our senses.*

Say 1 Our Father.

Scripture Text

Say 10 Hail Marys, each preceded by a text given below.

1. As soon as it was morning, the chief priests held a counsel with the elders and the scribes and the whole Sanhedrin.

2. They bound Jesus and led Him away, and handed Him over to Pilate.

3. Pilate asked Him, "Are You the King of the Jews?" Jesus replied, "You have said so."

4. Then the chief priests brought many charges against Him.

5. Again, Pilate questioned Him, "Have You no answer to offer? Just consider how many charges they are leveling against You." But Jesus offered no further reply, so that Pilate was amazed. . . .

6. The chief priests incited the crowd to have Pilate release Barabbas. . . . Pilate then asked, "And what shall I do with the Man you call King of the Jews?" They shouted back, "Crucify Him" (Mk 15:1-5, 11-14).

7. Pilate asked them, "Why? What evil has He done?" But they only screamed all the louder, "Crucify Him!"

8. A third time Pilate addressed them: "Why? What evil has He done? I have not found in Him any crime that deserves death. Therefore, I will have Him scourged and let Him go."

9. However, with loud shouts, they continued to insist that He should be crucified, and their voices prevailed. Pilate ordered that what they wanted was to be granted (Mk 23:22-24).

10. And so Pilate, anxious to appease the crowd, released Barabbas to them, and after handing Jesus over to be scourged, he gave Him over to be crucified (Mk 15:15).

Additional or Alternative Text

At the end of the first part of each Hail Mary after the Name "*Jesus*," add a few words that remind us of the Mystery being celebrated, as below. (The second part, "Holy Mary . . . ," is only recited once—at the end of the ten Hail Marys.)

(1) Who was the Suffering Servant of the Lord. (2) Who was unjustly slapped by a guard in the house of Caiaphas. (3) Who was denied three times by the future head of His Church. (4) Who endured humiliation at the hands of Herod. (5) Who was stripped of His clothes. (6) Who suffered scorn and insults from His captors because of His nakedness. (7) Who was beaten and tortured with sharp rods and ruthless whips. (8) Who was tied to a pillar. (9) Who shed blood and received injuries to His flesh. (10) Who collapsed out of weakness into a puddle of His own blood.

Say 1 Glory Be to the Father.

May the grace of our Lord's Scourging come down into my soul and make me truly mortified.

"O my Jesus," etc., p. 61.

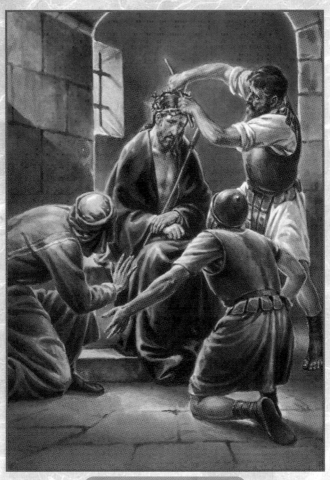

Crowning with Thorns

◖ Crowning with Thorns ◗

I Desire Moral Courage

Reflection

Think of the crown of sharp thorns that was forced upon our Lord's sacred Head and the patience with which He endured the pain for our sins.

Participation

1 Our Father.   10 Hail Marys.
1 Glory Be to the Father.

Prayer

Jesus, You patiently endured the pain from the crown of sharp thorns that was forced upon Your Head. Grant me the strength to have *moral courage*.

"O my Jesus, forgive us our sins, save us from the fire of hell, take all souls to heaven, and help especially those most in need of Your mercy."

Prayer

Lord Jesus, we offer You this third decade to honor Your Crowning with Thorns, and we ask of You, through this Mystery and through the intercession of Your Holy Mother, *the grace of moral courage.*

Say 1 Our Father.

Scripture Text

Say 10 Hail Marys, each preceded by a text given below.

1. The soldiers led Jesus away inside the palace, that is, the Praetorium, and they called the whole cohort together.

2. They dressed Him in a purple robe, and after twisting some thorns into a crown, they placed it on Him.

3. Then they began to salute Him with the words, "Hail, King of the Jews!"

4. They repeatedly struck His head with a reed, spat upon Him, and knelt before Him in homage (Mk 15:16-19).

5. Once again, Pilate went out and said to the Jews, "Look, I am bringing Him out to you to let you know that I find no evidence of a crime in Him."

6. Then Jesus came out wearing the Crown of Thorns and the Purple Robe, Pilate said to them, "Behold, the Man!"

7. When they saw Him, the chief priests and the Temple guards shouted, "Crucify Him! Crucify Him!" (Jn 19:4-6).

8. From that moment on, Pilate sought to release Him, but the people kept shouting, "If you release this

Man, you are no friend of Caesar. Every one who claims to be a king opposes Caesar."

9. When Pilate heard these words, he brought Jesus out and seated Him on the judge's bench at a place known as the Stone Pavement (in Hebrew, "Gabbatha"). . . . Pilate said to the Jews, "Behold, your King."

10. They shouted, "Away with Him! Away with Him! Crucify Him!" . . . "Am I to crucify your King?" Pilate asked them. The chief priests replied, "We have no king but Caesar." Then he handed Him over to be crucified (Jn 19:12-16).

Additional or Alternative Text

At the end of the first part of each Hail Mary after the Name "*Jesus*," add a few words that remind us of the Mystery being celebrated, as below. (The second part, "Holy Mary . . . ," is only recited once—at the end of the ten Hail Marys.)

(1) Who was undressed for a third time. (2) Who was given a crown of thorns on His Head. (3) Who was blindfolded with a veil. (4) Who endured the blows and the spittle from those whom He could not see. (5) Around Whose shoulders an old robe was thrown. (6) In Whose hand a reed was thrust. (7) Who was spit upon and insulted. (8) Who had abuses and insults hurled at Him. (9) Who had blood streaming from His adorable head. (10) Who was the image of a man defiled by sin.

Say 1 Glory Be to the Father.

May the grace of the Mystery of our Lord's Crowning with Thorns come down into my soul and help me to have moral courage.

"O my Jesus," etc., p. 61.

Carrying of the Cross

⸎ Carrying of the Cross ⸎

I Desire the Virtue of Patience

Reflection

Think of the heavy Cross, so willingly carried by our Lord, and ask Him to help you to carry your crosses without complaint.

Participation

1 Our Father.   10 Hail Marys.
1 Glory Be to the Father.

Prayer

Jesus, You willingly carried Your Cross for love of Your Father and all people. Grant me the *virtue of patience*.

"O my Jesus, forgive us our sins, save us from the fire of hell, take all souls to heaven, and help especially those most in need of Your mercy."

Prayer

Lord Jesus, we offer You this fourth decade to honor Your Carrying of the Cross, and we ask of You, through this Mystery and through the intercession of Your Holy Mother, *great patience in carrying our cross in Your footsteps every day.*

Say 1 Our Father.

Scripture Text

Say 10 Hail Marys, each preceded by a text given below.

1. When they had finished mocking Jesus, they stripped Him of the robe, dressed Him in His own clothes, and led Him away to crucify Him.

2. As they went out, they encountered a man from Cyrene named Simon, and they forced him to carry the Cross (Mt 27:31-32).

3. A large number of people followed Jesus, among them many women who were mourning and lamenting over Him.

4. But He turned to them and said, "Daughters of Jerusalem, do not weep for Me. Weep rather for yourselves and for your children" (Lk 23:27-28).

5. There were also two others, both criminals, who were led away to be executed with Him (Lk 23:32).

6. When they came to a place called Golgotha, which means the Place of the Skull, they offered Him some wine to drink that had been mixed with gall, but after tasting it, He refused to drink the mixture.

7. And after they had crucified Him, they divided His garments among them by casting lots. Then they sat down there to keep guard over Him.

8. Above His Head was inscribed the charge against Him: "This is Jesus, the King of the Jews."

9. Two thieves were crucified with Him, one on His right and the other on His left.

10. Those people who passed by jeered at Him, shaking their heads and saying, "You who claimed You could destroy the Temple and rebuild it within three days, save Yourself! If You truly are the Son of God, come down from the Cross" (Mt 27:33-40).

Additional or Alternative Text

At the end of the first part of each Hail Mary after the Name *"Jesus,"* add a few words that remind us of the Mystery being celebrated, as below. (The second part, "Holy Mary . . . ," is only recited once—at the end of the ten Hail Marys.)

(1) Who was presented to the people with the words: "Behold, the Man!" (2) Who was condemned for our sins. (3) Who carried the Cross to Calvary. (4) Whose Cross the good Cyrenian helped to carry. (5) Who was comforted by the pious women. (6) Who was whipped by the soldiers as He walked. (7) Who, by falling, atoned for our falls. (8) Who had a sorrowful meeting with you, His Mother. (9) Who left an imprint of His countenance on Veronica's veil. (10) Who indicates the way of salvation.

Say 1 Glory Be to the Father.

May the grace of the Mystery of the Carrying of the Cross come down into my soul and make me truly patient in carrying my crosses.

"O my Jesus," etc., p. 61.

The Crucifixion

❧ The Crucifixion ☙

I Desire the Grace of Final Perseverance

Reflection

Think of the love that filled Christ's Sacred Heart during His three hours' agony on the Cross, and ask Him to be with you at the hour of death.

Participation

1 Our Father.   10 Hail Marys.
1 Glory Be to the Father.

Prayer

Jesus, for love of me You endured three hours of torture on the Cross and gave up Your Spirit. Grant me the grace of *final perseverance.*

"O my Jesus, forgive us our sins, save us from the fire of hell, take all souls to heaven, and help especially those most in need of Your mercy."

5. THE CRUCIFIXION—LONG VERSION

> ## Prayer
>
> **Lord Jesus, we offer You this fifth decade to honor Your Crucifixion on Mount Calvary, and we ask of You, through this Mystery and through the intercession of Your Holy Mother, the *grace of final perseverance*.**

Say 1 Our Father.

Scripture Text

Say 10 Hail Marys, each preceded by a text given below.

1. Jesus said, "Father forgive them, for they do not know what they are doing" (Lk 23:34).

2. One of the criminals said, "Jesus, remember me when You come into Your Kingdom." Jesus said to him, "Amen, I say to you, today you will be with Me in Paradise" (Lk 23:42-43).

3. When Jesus saw His Mother and the disciple whom He loved standing beside her, He said to His Mother, "Woman, behold, your son." Then He said to the disciple, "Behold, your mother." And from that hour the disciple took her into his home (Jn 19:26-27).

4. About three o'clock, Jesus cried out . . . "My God, My God, why have You forsaken Me?" (Mt 27:46).

5. In order that the Scripture might be fulfilled, Jesus said, "I thirst." . . . They soaked a sponge in the wine on a branch of hyssop and held it up to His lips.

6. When Jesus had taken the wine He said, "It is finished" (Jn 19:28-30).

7. It was now about noon, and darkness came over the whole land until three in the afternoon, for the sun was

darkened. Then the veil of the Temple was torn in two. Jesus cried out, "Father, into Your hands I commend My spirit." And with these words He expired (Lk 23:45-46).

8. When the soldiers came to Jesus and saw that He was already dead, they did not break His legs, but one of the soldiers thrust a lance into His side, and immediately a flow of blood and water came forth (Jn 19:33-34).

9. They took the body of Jesus and wrapped it with the spices in linen cloths, according to Jewish custom.

10. At the place where Jesus had been crucified there was a garden with a new tomb in which no one had ever been buried. So they laid Jesus there (Jn 19:41-42).

Additional or Alternative Text

At the end of the first part of each Hail Mary after the Name "*Jesus*," add a few words that remind us of the Mystery being celebrated, as below. (The second part, "Holy Mary . . . ," is only recited once—at the end of the ten Hail Marys.)

(1) Who was crucified on Mount Calvary. (2) Who experienced shame and disgrace by being crucified naked between two robbers. (3) Who asked pardon for those who killed Him. (4) Who was aided by your compassion. (5) Who said seven last words from the Cross. (6) Who promised Paradise to the good thief. (7) Whose death caused the distress of the entire universe. (8) Who was taken down from the Cross and buried. (9) Whom you offered to the Father on the altar of the Cross. (10) Who renews His sacrifice at every Mass.

Say 1 Glory Be to the Father.

May the grace of the Mystery of the Passion and Death of our Lord and Savior Jesus Christ come down into my soul and obtain for me final perseverance.

"O my Jesus," etc., p. 61.

1. The Resurrection

2. The Ascension

3. The Descent of
the Holy Spirit

4. The Assumption

5. The Coronation of the BVM

The Five
Glorious Mysteries

*The Glorious Mysteries recall to our mind
the ratification of Christ's sacrifice for the
redemption of the world, and our sharing
in the fruits of His sacrifice*

The Resurrection

◖The Resurrection◗

I Desire a Strong Faith

Reflection

Think of Christ's glorious triumph when, on the third day after His death, He arose from the tomb and for forty days appeared to His Blessed Mother and to His disciples.

Participation

1 Our Father.   10 Hail Marys.
1 Glory Be to the Father.

Prayer

Jesus, You rose from the dead in triumph and remained for forty days with Your disciples, instructing and encouraging them. Increase my *faith*.

*"O my Jesus, forgive us our sins, save us from the fire of hell, take all souls to heaven, and help especially those most in need of Your mercy."

*In her second apparition at Fatima, June 13, 1917, our Lady taught three shepherd children to add this invocation after each decade of the Rosary.

Prayer

Lord Jesus, we offer You this first decade to honor Your glorious Resurrection, and we ask of You, through this Mystery and through the intercession of Your Holy Mother, *a strong faith.*

Say 1 Our Father.

Scripture Text

Say 10 Hail Marys, each preceded by a text given below.

1. At dawn on the first day of the week, Mary Magdalene and the other Mary went to visit the sepulcher.

2. And behold, there was a violent earthquake, for an Angel of the Lord, descended from heaven, came and rolled back the stone and sat upon it. His face shone like lightning, and his garments were as white as snow.

3. The guards were so paralyzed with fear of him that they became like dead men.

4. But the Angel said to the women, "Do not be afraid! I know that you are looking for Jesus, Who was crucified. He is not here, for He has been raised as He promised.

5. "Come and see the place where He lay. Then go and tell His disciples: 'He has been raised from the dead and now He is going ahead of you to Galilee. There you will see Him.' Behold, I have told you" (Mt 28:1-7).

6. The disciples were filled with joy when they saw the Lord. "Peace be with you," Jesus said to them. "As the Father has sent Me, so I send you."

7. He breathed on them and said, "Receive the Holy Spirit. If you forgive anyone's sins, they are forgiven. If you retain anyone's sins, they are retained." . . .

8. When the other disciples told Thomas, "We have seen the Lord," he replied, "Unless I see the mark of the nails on His hands and put my finger into the place where the nails pierced and insert my hand into His side, I will not believe."
. . .

9. "Jesus said to Thomas, "Put your finger here and see My hands. Reach out your hands and put it into My side. Do not doubt any longer, but believe."

10. Thomas exclaimed, "My Lord and my God!" Then Jesus said to him, "You have come to believe because you have seen Me. Blessed are those who have not seen and yet have come to believe" (Jn 20:20-25, 27-29).

Additional or Alternative Text

At the end of the first part of each Hail Mary after the Name "*Jesus*," add a few words that remind us of the Mystery being celebrated, as below. (The second part, "Holy Mary . . . ," is only recited once—at the end of the ten Hail Marys.)

(1) Who rose from the dead on the third day. (2) Who obtained a victory over death, sin, the world, and the devil. (3) Who appeared to His holy Mother, the Apostles, and the disciples. (4) Who gave the Apostles the power to forgive sins. (5) Who broke bread with the pilgrims of Emmaus. (6) Who revealed to Thomas the blessedness of belief. (7) Who renews Easter in every Eucharist. (8) Who rises in the hearts of those who do penance. (9) Who always dies and rises again in the Church. (10) Who is the Firstfruits of our resurrection.

Say 1 Glory Be to the Father.

May the grace of the Resurrection come down into my soul and make me strong in faith.

"O my Jesus," etc., p. 83.

The Ascension

❧ The Ascension ☙

I Desire the Virtue of Hope

Reflection

Think of the Ascension of Jesus Christ, forty days after His glorious Resurrection, in the presence of Mary and His disciples.

Participation

1 Our Father.   10 Hail Marys.
1 Glory Be to the Father.

Prayer

Jesus, in the presence of Mary and the disciples You ascended to heaven to sit at the Father's Right Hand. Increase the *virtue of hope in me.*

"O my Jesus, forgive us our sins, save us from the fire of hell, take all souls to heaven, and help especially those most in need of Your mercy."

Prayer

Lord Jesus, we offer You this second decade to honor Your glorious Ascension, and we ask of You, through this Mystery and through Mary's intercession, *a firm hope and a deep longing for heaven.*

Say 1 Our Father.

Scripture Text

Say 10 Hail Marys, each preceded by a text given below.

1. Jesus led His disciples as far as Bethany, and lifting up His hands, He blessed them (Lk 24:50).

2. Jesus said, "All authority in heaven and on earth has been given to Me.

3. "Go, therefore, and make disciples of all nations, baptizing them in the Name of the Father and of the Son and of the Holy Spirit, and teaching them to observe all that I have commanded you.

4. "And behold, I am with you always, to the end of the world" (Mt 28:18-20).

5. "Whoever believes and is baptized will be saved; whoever does not believe will be condemned" (Mk 16:16).

6. While Jesus was blessing them, He departed from them and was taken up to heaven (Lk 24:51).

7. While He was departing as they gazed upward toward the sky, suddenly two men dressed in white robes stood beside them.

8. "Men of Galilee, why are you standing there looking up into the sky? This Jesus Who has been taken up from you into heaven will come back in the same way

as you have seen Him going into heaven" (Acts 1:10-11).

9. They worshiped Jesus and then returned to Jerusalem filled with great joy, and they were continually in the Temple praising God (Lk 24:52-53).

10. Jesus took His place at the right hand of God (Mk 16:20).

Additional or Alternative Text

At the end of the first part of each Hail Mary after the Name "Jesus," add a few words that remind us of the Mystery being celebrated, as below. (The second part, "Holy Mary . . . ," is only recited once—at the end of the ten Hail Marys.)

(1) Who as Risen Lord spent forty days with His disciples, teaching them many things. (2) Who met with all His disciples on the Mount of Olives. (3) Who imparted a blessing on them as He was rising from the earth to heaven. (4) Who ascended into heaven by virtue of His own power. (5) Who received a welcome and divine triumph by His Father and by the whole celestial assembly. (6) Who opened the gates of heaven. (7) Who is enthroned at the right hand of the Father as His Beloved Son, equal to Him. (8) Who received the power to judge the living and the dead. (9) Who watches over our journey. (10) Who has promised to remain with us forever.

Say 1 Glory Be to the Father.

May the grace of the Mystery of the Ascension come down into my soul and give me strong hope.

"O my Jesus," etc., p. 83.

The Descent of the Holy Spirit

❧ The Descent of ❧ the Holy Spirit

I Desire Zeal for the Glory of God

Reflection

Think of the Descent of the Holy Spirit upon Mary and the Apostles, under the form of tongues of fire, in fulfillment of Christ's promise.

Participation

1 Our Father.   10 Hail Marys.
1 Glory Be to the Father.

Prayer

Jesus, in fulfillment of Your promise You sent the Holy Spirit upon Mary and the disciples under the form of tongues of fire. *Increase my zeal for God's glory.*

"O my Jesus, forgive us our sins, save us from the fire of hell, take all souls to heaven, and help especially those most in need of Your mercy."

Prayer

Holy Spirit, we offer You this third decade to honor Your Descent on Pentecost and we ask of You, through this Mystery and through the intercession of Mary, Your most faithful Spouse, *zeal and love for the glory of God.*

Say 1 Our Father.

Scripture Text

Say 10 Hail Marys, each preceded by a text given below.

1. "The Advocate, the Holy Spirit, Whom the Father will send in My Name will teach you everything and remind you of all that I have said to you" (Jn 14:26).

2. "Within a few days you will be baptized with the Holy Spirit. . . ."

3. "You will receive power when the Holy Spirit comes upon you, and then you will be My witnesses not only in Jerusalem, but throughout Judea and Samaria, and indeed to the farthest ends of the earth" (Acts 1:5, 8).

4. When the day of Pentecost arrived, they were all assembled together in one place.

5. Suddenly, there came from heaven a sound similar to that of a violent wind, and it filled the entire house in which they were sitting.

6. Then there appeared to them tongues of fire, which separated and came to rest on each one of them. All of them were filled with the Holy Spirit and began to speak in different languages as the Spirit enabled them to do.

7. Now staying in Jerusalem there were devout Jews from every nation under heaven. At this sound, a large

crowd of them gathered, and they were bewildered because each one heard them speaking in his own language (Acts 2:1-6).

8. Peter said, "Repent, and be baptized every one of you, in the Name of Jesus Christ, so that your sins may be forgiven, and you will receive the gift of the Holy Spirit.

9. "For the promise that was made is for you, for your children, and for all those who are far away, for all those whom the Lord our God will call" (Acts 2:38-39).

10. Those who accepted His message were baptized, and on that day about three thousand people were added to their number (Acts 2:41).

Additional or Alternative Text

At the end of the first part of each Hail Mary after the Name "*Jesus,*" add a few words that remind us of the Mystery being celebrated, as below. (The second part, "Holy Mary . . . ," is only recited once—at the end of the ten Hail Marys.)

(1) Who with the Father sent the Holy Spirit upon His followers. (2) Who transformed the disciples into Apostles. (3) Who consecrated you as "Mother of the Church." (4) Who always enriches the Church with charisms. (5) Who consecrates those who are baptized and confirms them in their faith. (6) Who consecrates ministers for service to the community. (7) Who consecrates those who are called to perfect charity. (8) Who consecrates those who are married for the ministry of life. (9) Who always inspires His followers. (10) Who consecrates and preserves the goods of creation.

Say 1 Glory Be to the Father.

May the grace of Pentecost come down into my soul and inspire me to have zeal for the glory of God.

"O my Jesus," etc., p. 83.

The Assumption

❦ The Assumption ❧

I Desire Grace of a Holy Death

Reflection

Think of the glorious Assumption of Mary into Heaven, when she was reunited with her Divine Son.

Participation

1 Our Father.   10 Hail Marys.
1 Glory Be to the Father.

Prayer

Mary, by the power of God you were assumed into heaven and reunited with your Divine Son. Help me to have the *gift of a holy death*.

"O my Jesus, forgive us our sins, save us from the fire of hell, take all souls to heaven, and help especially those most in need of Your mercy."

Prayer

Lord Jesus, we offer You this fourth decade to honor the Assumption of Your Holy Mother, body and soul, into heaven, and we ask of You, through this Mystery and through her intercession, the *gift of a holy death*.

Say 1 Our Father.

Scripture Text

Say 10 Hail Marys, each preceded by a text given below.

1. The Lord God said to the serpent, "I will put enmity between you and the Woman, and between your offspring and hers.

2. "He will strike at your head, while you strike at His heel" (Gen 3:15).

3. A great sign appeared in heaven: a Woman clothed with the sun, with the moon beneath her feet, and a crown of twelve stars on her head (Rev 12:1).

4. My daughter, listen carefully to my words and follow them diligently. Forget not your people and your father's house; then the king will desire your beauty. Since He is your Lord, bow down before Him (Ps 45:11-13).

5. "Your deed of hope will never be forgotten by those who tell of the might of God.

6. "May God make this redound to Your everlasting honor, rewarding You with blessings . . . walking upright before our God" (Jud 13:18-20).

7. "You are the glory of Jerusalem, the surpassing joy of Israel; You are the splendid boast of our people" (Jud 15:9-10).

8. "Who is this that comes forth like the dawn, as beautiful as the moon, as resplendent as the sun, awe-inspiring as bannered troops?" (Song 6:10).

9. "Those who love me, I also love, and those who seek me find me. . . . He who finds me finds life and wins favor from the Lord" (Prov 8:17, 35).

10. All honor to you, Mary! Today you were raised above the choirs of Angels to lasting glory with Christ (*Feast of Assumption*).

Additional or Alternative Text

At the end of the first part of each Hail Mary after the Name "Jesus," add a few words that remind us of the Mystery being celebrated, as below. (The second part, "Holy Mary . . . ," is only recited once—at the end of the ten Hail Marys.)

(1) Who took you to heaven by your Assumption. (2) Who associated you in His Resurrection. (3) Who glorified your humanity. (4) Who exalted your humility. (5) Who rejoices in your Motherhood. (6) Who rewarded your virginity. (7) Who exalts you as the Mother of the Church. (8) Who constituted you as the type of the glorified Church. (9) Who inspires in us the hope of a happy death. (10) Who inspires in us the desire for eternal happiness.

Say 1 Glory Be to the Father.

May the grace of the Mystery of the Assumption come down into my soul and enable me to have a holy death.

"O my Jesus," etc., p. 83.

The Coronation of the Blessed Virgin Mary

❦ The Coronation of the ❧ Blessed Virgin Mary

I Desire a Greater Love for the Blessed Virgin Mary

Reflection

Think of the glorious Crowning of Mary as Queen of Heaven by her Divine Son, to the great joy of all the Saints.

Participation

1 Our Father.   10 Hail Marys.
1 Glory Be to the Father.

Prayer

Mary, you were crowned Queen of Heaven by your Divine Son to the great joy of all the Saints. Obtain for me *greater love for you.*

"O my Jesus, forgive us our sins, save us from the fire of hell, take all souls to heaven, and help especially those most in need of Your mercy."

Prayer

Lord Jesus, we offer You this fifth decade to honor the Glorious Crowning of Your Holy Mother in heaven, and we ask of You, through this Mystery and through her intercession, *a greater love for the Blessed Virgin Mary.*

Say 1 Our Father.

Scripture Text

Say 10 Hail Marys, each preceded by a text given below.

1. Daughters of kings are among Your women in waiting; at Your right hand is Your Queen adorned in gold of Ophir. Within the palace the King's daughter is adorned in robes threaded with gold. In embroidered garments she is led to the king, followed by her virgin companions, who are also led to You (Ps 45:10, 14-15).

2. My heart is moved by a noble theme as I sing my poem to the king (Ps 45:2).

3. You are the most handsome of men; grace has anointed Your lips, for God has blessed You forever (Ps 45:3).

4. I rejoice greatly in the Lord, in my God is the joy of my soul. For He has clothed me with a robe of salvation, wrapped me in a mantle of justice, like a bright broom adorned with a diadem, like a bride bedecked with her jewels (Isa 61:10).

5. "My soul proclaims the greatness of the Lord and my spirit rejoices in God my Savior.

6. "For He has looked with favor on the lowliness of His servant; henceforth all generations will call me blessed.

7. "The Mighty One has done great things for me, and holy is His Name" (Lk 1:46-49).

8. Mary, ever-virgin, most honored Queen of the world, you gave birth to our Savior, Christ the Lord (*Queenship of Mary*).

9. Blessed are you, Virgin Mary, because you believed that the Lord's words to you would be fulfilled; now you reign with Christ for ever (*Queenship of Mary*).

10. Come, let us worship Christ Who crowned His Mother as Queen of heaven and earth (*Queenship of Mary*).

Additional or Alternative Text

At the end of the first part of each Hail Mary after the Name "Jesus," add a few words that remind us of the Mystery being celebrated, as below. (The second part, "Holy Mary . . . ," is only recited once—at the end of the ten Hail Marys.)

(1) Who placed a crown on you in heaven. (2) Who associated you in His Royalty. (3) Who chose you as Queen of the Universe. (4) Who associated you in His universal mediation. (5) Who constituted you Mother of Mercy. (6) Who chose you as Queen of Patriarchs and Prophets. (7) Who made you Queen of Martyrs and Virgins. (8) Who constituted you Queen of Apostles and Missionaries. (9) Who chose you as Queen of Peace. (10) Who constituted you the Maternal Sovereign of all peoples.

Say 1 Glory Be to the Father.

May the grace of the Mystery of the Crowning of Your Holy Mother come down into my soul and inspire me to have greater love for the Blessed Virgin Mary.

"O my Jesus," etc., p. 83.

PRAYER AFTER THE ROSARY

O GOD, Whose, only-begotten Son, by His Life, Death, and Resurrection, has purchased for us the rewards of eternal life; grant, we beseech You, that, meditating upon these Mysteries of the Most Holy Rosary of the Blessed Virgin Mary, we may imitate what they contain and obtain what they promise, through the same Christ our Lord. Amen.

℣. May the divine assistance remain always with us. ℟. Amen.

℣. And may the souls of the faithful departed, through the mercy of God, rest in peace. ℟. Amen.

THE PRAYERS OF THE ROSARY

The Our Father

OUR Father, Who art in heaven, hallowed be Thy name; Thy kingdom come; Thy will be done on earth as it is in heaven. Give us this day our daily bread; and forgive us our trespasses as we forgive those who trespass against us; and lead us not into temptation, but deliver us from evil. Amen.

The Hail Mary

HAIL Mary, full of grace, the Lord is with you; blessed are you among women, and blessed is the fruit of your womb, Jesus. Holy Mary, Mother of God, pray for us sinners now and at the hour of our death. Amen.

Glory Be to the Father

GLORY be to the Father, and to the Son, and to the Holy Spirit. As it was in the beginning, is now, and ever shall be, world without end. Amen.

The Apostles' Creed

I BELIEVE in God, the Father Almighty, Creator of heaven and earth; and in Jesus Christ, His only Son, our Lord; Who was conceived by the Holy Spirit, born of the Virgin Mary, suffered under Pontius Pilate, was crucified, died and was buried. He descended into hell; the third day He arose again from the dead; He ascended into heaven, and sits at the right hand of God, the Father Almighty; from thence He shall come to judge the living and the dead. I believe in the Holy Spirit, the Holy Catholic Church, the communion of saints, the forgiveness of sins, the resurrection of the body, and life everlasting. Amen.

The Hail! Holy Queen

HAIL! Holy Queen, Mother of Mercy, our life, our sweetness, and our hope. To you do we cry, poor banished children of Eve. To you do we send up our sighs, mourning and weeping in this valley of tears. Turn then, O most gracious advocate, your eyes of mercy toward us; and after this our exile, show unto us the blessed fruit of your womb, Jesus. O clement! O loving! O sweet Virgin Mary!

℣. Pray for us, O Holy Mother of God. ℟. That we may be made worthy of the promises of Christ.

The Litany of Loreto

Lord, have mercy.
Christ, have mercy.
Lord, have mercy.
Christ, hear us.
Christ, graciously hear us.
God, the Father of heaven,
   have mercy on us.
God, the Son, Redeemer of the
   world,
   have mercy on us.
God, the Holy Spirit,
   have mercy on us.
Holy Trinity, one God,
   have mercy on us.
Holy Mary, *pray for us.**
Holy Mother of God,
Holy Virgin of virgins,
Mother of Christ,
Mother of the Church,
Mother of Divine grace,
Mother most pure,
Mother most chaste,
Mother inviolate,
Mother undefiled,
Mother most amiable,
Mother most admirable,

Mother of good counsel,
Mother of our Creator,
Mother of our Savior,
Virgin most prudent,
Virgin most venerable,
Virgin most renowned,
Virgin most powerful,
Virgin most merciful,
Virgin most faithful,
Mirror of justice,
Seat of wisdom,
Cause of our joy,
Spiritual vessel,
Vessel of honor,
Singular vessel of devotion,
Mystical rose,
Tower of David,
Tower of ivory,
House of gold,
Ark of the covenant,
Gate of heaven,
Morning star,
Health of the sick,
Refuge of sinners,
Comforter of the afflicted,
Help of Christians,

* *Pray for us* is repeated after each invocation.

The Litany of Loreto

Queen of angels,
Queen of patriarchs,
Queen of prophets,
Queen of apostles,
Queen of martyrs,
Queen of confessors,
Queen of virgins,
Queen of all saints,
Queen conceived without original sin,
Queen assumed into heaven,
Queen of the most holy Rosary,
Queen of families,
Queen of peace,

Lamb of God, You take away the sins of the world; *spare us, O Lord!*

Lamb of God, You take away the sins of the world; *graciously hear us, O Lord!*

Lamb of God, You take away the sins of the world; *have mercy on us.*

℣. Pray for us, O holy Mother of God.

℟. *That we may be made worthy of the promises of Christ.*

*L*ET us pray.
Grant, we beg You, O Lord God,
that we Your servants
may enjoy lasting health of mind and body,
and by the glorious intercession
of the Blessed Mary, ever Virgin,
be delivered from present sorrow
and enter into the joy of eternal happiness.
Through Christ our Lord.
℟. *Amen.*

Prayer to Our Lady of the Rosary

MARY, Queen of the Holy Rosary,
your Divine Son Jesus is the perfect
Mediator
between God and human beings,
because He alone could in all justice merit
our reconciliation with God
as well as the graces that God would impart
after the reconciliation.
You are the Mediatrix in union with Christ
from Whom your mediation draws all its
power.
You merited the title of Unique Associate
above all by your union with Christ
in His redemptive sacrifice.

After Jesus, no one suffered as you did.
Now your action is primarily one of intercession.
In your contemplation of God,
you behold our needs with our prayers
and you beg God to grant these favors.

May the faithful recitation of my Rosary
be a sign of my gratitude to Jesus and to you
for all you have done for me
in bringing about my Redemption.
May my Rosary also be a means
of obtaining all the graces I need
for the sanctification and salvation of my
soul.

THE FIVE NEW LUMINOUS MYSTERIES

ON October 16, 2002, Pope John Paul II issued an Apostolic Letter entitled The *Rosary of the Virgin Mary*, encouraging all Catholics to recite the Rosary. He also suggested five new Mysteries that might supplement the meditation on the traditional Joyful, Sorrowful, and Glorious Mysteries of the Rosary.

The new Mysteries, i.e., Mysteries of Light or the Luminous Mysteries, are intended to offer contemplation of important parts of Christ's Public Life in addition to the contemplation on His Childhood, His Sufferings, and His Risen Life offered by the traditional Mysteries: "Of the many Mysteries of Christ's life, only a few are indicated by the Rosary in the form that has become generally established with the seal of the Church's approval. . . .

"I believe, however, that to bring out fully the Christological depth of the Rosary it would be suitable to make an addition to the traditional pattern which, while left to the freedom of individuals and communities, could broaden it to include the Mysteries of Christ's Public Ministry between His

Baptism and His Passion. In the course of those Mysteries we contemplate important aspects of the person of Christ as the definitive revelation of God. Declared the beloved Son of the Father at the Baptism in the Jordan, Christ is the One Who announces the coming of the Kingdom, bears witness to it in His works and proclaims its demands. It is during the years of His Public Ministry that the Mystery of Christ is most evidently a Mystery of Light: 'While I am in the world, I am the light of the world' (Jn 9:5).

"Consequently . . . it is fitting to add, following reflection on the Incarnation and the Hidden Life of Christ (the Joyful Mysteries) and before focusing on the sufferings of His Passion (the Sorrowful Mysteries) and the triumph of His Resurrection (the Glorious Mysteries), a meditation on certain particularly significant moments in His Public Ministry (the Mysteries of Light)."

The Pope assigned these new Mysteries to Thursday while transferring the Joyful Mysteries—normally said on that day—to Saturday because of the special Marian presence in them.